GW00566758

Moon for Sale

RICHARD PRICE

CARCANET

First published in Great Britain in 2017 by
Carcanet Press Ltd
Alliance House, 30 Cross Street
Manchester M2 7AQ
www.carcanet.co.uk

A CIP catalogue record for this book is available
from the British Library, ISBN 9781784102845

Typeset by XL Publishing Services, Exmouth
Printed & bound in England by SRP Ltd.

The publisher acknowledges financial assistance
from Arts Council England.

CONTENTS

Look, the bright full moon
is the town clock, its dark hands
missing, robbed for scrap.

This is how a book could be –
tonight it's ballet, tomorrow
apply a different progression code
within the hyperlex transfer protocol.

There'll be a future name for a flicker render, mimicking film.
It's fine, you can theorise in poetry,
sing analysis in. There's lyric in the language of the intellect –
lyric can be intelligent, breathing out a thought, attentive adoration.

This is how a page could be –
mostly white space for the text wall, and the windows varying in size, varied in shape,
colour saturation, force of light.
It is all dancing and stage-build today, rich reds by design,
but you can still cherish resolving in the eye / hands.

Tomorrow this is how pauses work

This is how ellipses…
and now dashes –
          positioning, movement
                              and you make it all a performance –
Would you like to buy this programme?

(The contents resemble everything I once wanted, worked for, resemble…
nothing you could have seen before,

                         and now they're all alight.)

Remember when a poem could be banned
        for beginning with the word 'Remember'? –
for mentioning it was a poem,
for bearing the weight of twenty-three syllables
        on the long oak bough of any given line?

(Those tiny birds, conspiring on the other side of that branch,
had to be counted.
No modulated breath was safe, no high canopy.)

Remember when a poem could be censured for exaggerating –
        using that juvenile word 'banned', for example –
 simplifying 'exactly', or displaying 'exotic lite', deploying 'marram',
'palimpsest', or 'shard'?

I loved those years.
I am a Trading Standards Officer.
There should be a price on every word.

Play gentle, Rich, play nice.
You'll always be
        a government inspector.
You'll always be a —

I had a key for everything then, real keys and metaphorical.
Data Protection was my brief –
Magnúsdóttir, since you ask, Lacock, and bacon.
(I can say nothing regarding parentage but may I suggest
a widening of your diet, a little more adventure in your travel?
Questions for password amnesia don't require authenticity –
the psy-ops mantra is 'persistence of the identifier, not reality in identity'.
If you have to stay local, there's always Io or Brigadoon.

Play gentle, Rich, play nice.
You'll always be
        a quantity surveyor.
You'll always be a —

My favourite key, real, had the heft of a tenon saw –
(I feel we'd better have a word like 'heft' in this well-crafted poem,
we all need a guarantee, the reassurance of heritage vocabulary,
and consensus in the first-person plural).
That implement liberated a certain opening in the old king's demesne,
a gate in a small postern.
It was all-weather but bore a delicate emblem:
on one half of the shield there was a furious dragon,
on the other judging balances, for the measurement of pie-wrens or hashish.
Each device was fading black on a field of deep red.
Through the warped door the forbidden forest
        must still luxuriate in the complex anthem
of leaf drip, mammal call, a soft baffling of breezes, mystery percussion.
The birds grumble but I tell you they can be decoded.)

Play gentle, Rich, play nice.
You'll always be
        a debt collector.
You'll always be a —

Oh you've lost that little padlock from your charm bracelet.
(As this is a poem I'll just say what you already know –
let our listeners glean a little more private information for next to nothing,
actually it's all on me.)
That silver safeguard was also a freebie,
the shining plummet from a rent but unexploded cracker.
Our first get-together was a Christmas burlesque in the heat of summer:
out amid the *marram* the pom-pom hats didn't stay on for long
and you cut yourself on a Viking, on a Viking *shard*

(a piece of jagged plastic from some ready-meal packaging,
and the *palimpsest* in the digitised object says the provenance is I-c-e-l-a-n-d).

Play gentle, Rich, play nice.
You'll always be
      a lie detector.
You'll always be a —

Months later – here I'll continue to explain what you already know,
     it's only polite when we have company –
you agreed with a kiss you'd accept a binding contract.
It was actually winter but the heating warranted shorts.
We'd never settled for the takeover of sharing my name.
We'd always understood we'd be equals
       under differentiated language –
and let any children choose their own ropeways.

We registered our radical grafting but I'm afraid this poem isn't permitted
to clamber up anyone else's family tree,
or slip down I should say, since, like the inverted offering of Seahenge,
we are surely all in descent, the lowest tips yet in humanity's burial darkness.

Play gentle, Rich, play nice.
You'll always be
      a coin curator.
You'll always be a —

I like a good ghost story. I know the cost of the arboretum.
I'm sorry we taught each other
     to specialise in adjustments of loss.
It's no good saying now I couldn't have known I was an expert
in short-selling, owned nothing I would risk,
    that I borrowed security from your promise and still
    bless the profit of our hopes – not quite held, certainly sold.

Play gentle, Rich, play nice.

A gap appears during the act of valuation:
value is an anxious covering, not an estimation of the ontic.

Play gentle, Rich, play nice.
You'll always be
        a ready reckoner.
You'll always be a —

There is a cost to fervour, adulation.
There is a cost to measure, to calculation. There is a cost…
There is a cost to conclusion –
you can surely hear now how this text is slowing,
it has sighted the deal, its destination.
I can sense you welcome the farewell,
as I thought I detected, a little earlier, your exasperation –
this is a poem sinking with the pangs
        of the coming compromise, haggle completed,
the satisfactory simplicity of achieved dissatisfaction.
I should think there'd be some sort of repetition
at the finish, the poem's final handshake or set of receipts.
Capping a refrain's phrases can be quite effective? –
it's knowing, but I bet this poem will be trying to raise spirits.
Yes here it is, the finale, to be honest all suddenly sounding a bit rushed,
(*play gentle, Rich, play nice*)
making a little rhyme of itself, self-obsessed to the last!

Play gentle, Rich, play nice.
You'll always be
        a loss adjustor.
You'll always be a Price.

The butterflies cash themselves in.
The little ones they call 'Coppers'
fall to earth – clink clink clink.

A collector's servants rake them off his lawns,
choke his little charity box.

Emperors and Admirals promise themselves into print.
Their wings convert, mid-air, into banknotes
and then they're caught in the slightest breeze,
snagged in hollybush and whitethorn.
They're the tatters of bunting – the cleaning contract was cancelled
on the day of the royal celebration.

The next scene I see – or feel, since seeing seems too distant a faculty –
is a sturdy till. It opens:
inside are butterfly fivers, butterfly tenners.
Little Blues and Large Blues are packed tight,
they're pinned down in brushed steel compartments
(sometimes with a hasp, sometimes with a spike).

The voice of my twin sister
(I do not have a twin sister)
says:

This is the work of the Hedge Funds
but the dream doesn't pulse like a joke.

The world brims, all brims,
and is the word 'choked'?

It would be simple —

Every leaf is painted by hand, green as new,

now darker,

    and reddish!,

  some

          golden?,

               falling.

I thought they were Labradors, too,
noses down, snuffling —
industrial wheelbarrows,
oxidised from mirror to autumn, —
two industrial wheelbarrows
way up there, at the works. Light

effects, distance.

(You knew, and whoever else, no problem.)

The word 'heart' and the word
'heartbroken' – but it's not
isolation, isolation

of vocab. Yes you can exist
artificially, says this headline,
full to limited capacity.

It's a way of way of life.

Get out of the car – I told you it would end this way.
Get out of the car – the satnav has nothing to say.

I wish *we* could talk
                    like the road whispers to the wheel.
I wish we could talk
                    like the dream
                              flirts
                                    with the real.

Motorway and track, motorway and track,
motorway, motorway, motorway.

I'll walk with you. The hill's the ocean floor.
I'll walk with you. I've been here, before.

I wish we could talk
                    like the sun soothes the gorse to bloom.
I wish we could talk
                    like the rocks
                              adore the moon.

Motorway and track, motorway and track,
motorway, motorway, motorway.

Get out the car –
I told you it would start this way.

Aching fern

All-of-a-sudden

Apocalypse daisy

Astonishment

Badgery

Banker's coke
See also Drone's wedding

Barochan's promise

Bee sigh

Boker

Bone

Bookbinder's ribbon

Bossgrip

Brags and droops

Brammer

Broch mallow

Bull sage

Carpet bomb *See also*
Immunity from prosecution

Clapshot

Climbing quarrel

Clype-of-the-field

Coarse squander

Cockspurt

Comeuppance

Common Sense

Control-Alt-Delete

Crannog herb

Dalston knotweed

Death spiral

Dentist's bib

Disappointment

Donkey's tickle

Drinker's Amen

Drone's wedding
See also Extraordinary rendition

Dwell on it

Edible squander

Eid basket

Electric nettle

Eton filth

Extraordinary rendition
See also Carpet bomb

Eyes on the heavens

Faithless

False Deuteronomy

False thistle

Fevergood

Fool's squander

Forgiveness

Freshwater lady

Fundament

Ginging

Gryffeweed

Hairy instructor

Honeysap

Immunity from prosecution
See also Banker's coke

Inkjet

Jenny's little problem

Justification

Kentigern's cress

Kilmacolm filigree

Lady's Adventure

Last Monarch

Lay-on-the-moss

Lord Randall's hope

Love Street lichen

Marshmoist

Moderation

Moist tuckweed

Moundly

Mouse parsley

Mrs Sailor's comfort

Neverblue

Now and then

The Now drug

Obelisker

Parable

Pauper's graphene

Pieces of moon

Poor man's magnet

Prickly maiden

Purple shoplifter

Quaker bonnet

Quimsly

Ragged Ritchie

Rancid poet

Roisterer's tip

St Fillan in the field

Sea clype

Sea lady

Sea smoke

Sea spunk

Selkie's nibble

Sell-by-dates

Shooshlove

SIM-leaf

Sloppy librarian

Sleep-by-my-side

Slip-it-in

Slip showing

Smooth instructor

Sniff of the rag

Snowrash

Soldermouth

Speedslow

Stamina

Stumblegrass

Sunprayer

Sweet Otis

Tailor's rescue

Telepathy

Tripvetch

Twicefold

Us-and-them

Venus vetch

Wetting themselves

Wolfeye

Wreckage forgetter

The X-ray plant

Yes-and-no

Zealot's secret

SNAILMAIL

for Peter Manson

Glisten of hand-drawn monorails, slopstream timelapse.
Rollercoaster tweenagers – helmets (oversize) slipped back.
The common or garden daredevil is approaching the speed of drool.

and the message is, and the message is

I was a spiral of scroll in a polished slipcase.
I was a lipcase. I was a lip.

I was illumination, initially,
seh seh security, mortality, in Mary's kitchen garden –
the children raced me, jabbed me.
Off-vellum, Mary's favourite dabbled then dictated – 'Now wash your hands.'

I was inked – the bruise from a signet ring. I was a signet ring.
I was marginalia on incunabula.
A silent type suckered me with sage, stamped my shell to test my blood.

and the message is, and the message is

I was a gastropod gargoyle –
I was dribbling yet more silver on the double-funded quad.
The kids weren't sluggish but they knew slime, grip, command.
I was a nest of *pain aux raisins*: stomach-foot was sweet-tooth,
built on cane, armoured, top of every crop.

I was persuasive, I was percussion – an *at* sign carbon-copying itself,
counting the cost in the sponsored hospitality suite,
devising mimeo verse with machines of pharmacists, secretaries and clerks.
I was the history of natural art, English as a foreign language,
I was the anti-school school mag, solemn and spiral binding.

and the message is, and the message is

I was a seamless body, a seamless bodysuit, with sci-fi backpack,
a he stroke she. 'You decide.'

Maybe there was something about the inner ear. I misheard it.
A circular argument.

I was open-cast mining, a land-tattoo as curse and naturalised utility.
'This squiggly jewellery is the best St Thomas' Day I've ever had.'

and the message is, and the message is

I was click-through, an email preposition –
where it's @, but never provably in.
I was a simple fractal, a future fossil –
I observed protocol, felt transfer in all good faith.
Daylight had to be saved: I kept nocturnal.
I cooked electric: I was garbage in, voltage out.

The world warms, but the human temperature is cooler.
Greed looms out of scale, beyond watch or word.
I am a lay observer, I am low, observed.
In sub-zero delirium I occupy yet a high aquarium
of frozen kiss and curve. I am a propagation of the absurd.

Still, this glass tank of baby tanks
('I find your reference to offensive offensive.')
will have its render: I'm angelic, a scream-
                                        saver.
Flicker after viscous flicker sleeks up on collateral children,

fixes their unfixable faces on their deadpan corpses.
I am slo-mo real time, as-if-perpetual,
forever dissolving in the weather in your area.

and the message is, and the message is
and the message, the message

and the message is, and the message is

denounced, devalued
(*delivered*).

Every shadow has a shadow.
In the dapple a dark speckle, the meadow's thirst.

Every sorrow has a sorrow,
a lessening lesson, a congealing ghost.

Density of loss:
a 'once was' (once was: brute finesse).

Grief, not grudge. Extinction's edge.
Last on the late last list.

There is a pang the weight of the sun's fist.
There is a pang the weight of the sun's fist.

Not that I'm saying anything,
at least, I'm more speaking just to be hearing, answering
to ask if *reply to reply* just might (not knowing)
perpetuate this pulse-on-pulse toing and froing,
as if here, in your here-and-now, is best brimmingness,
breathless, beyond fondness found.

Hard dream, extreme astound.
Death the sky, death the ground. Yet,
we're coming round.
We've been laughed alive,
paired-up for the dive, bound
to the vast unbound.

Let's swim in liquid sound, luxuriate
in while, in whim, in… flirt and secret flout,
It's not too late. Let doubts leave. For crying out loud
let's improvise our intimate lives, perfect an intricate duet.
Let's retrieve, in the whelm, in the depth,
kindness of touch – and, say, say this much:
we'll plan to play, to enjoy, stronger than belief, full sweet

'nothing' – if such pleasure (a kiss the gentlest of gentle decrees)
elicits your delicate, illicit *please.*

I think she likes

a little trouble, just a certain kind, a certain kind
of gentle trouble? (She doesn't need any trouble.)

There's a shape-shifter, a memory of an animal from a northern forest.
She's heard he was a finch. She's heard he was a fox.

There are wolves in the remains of the world –
some can howl and one of them can sing.
There's a pine marten the size of a man and it's not a pantomime suit
(maybe it is a pantomime suit).

She's a shape-shifter herself, a swimmer, a time-traveller, she's Modern Dance.

(The kind of trouble that's no trouble, a finger
tracing a tattoo

on soft skin).

The feathered creatures disturb her dreams.
As black as ash a harsh bird roosts on the little balcony.
It's a large rock, it's a punishment of a bible.
It defies her. She throws cigarette packets
but it doesn't flinch.

How can you give up smoking
when a harsh bird is nesting on the balcony?

It's a harsh bird, but it's a family bird:
that charcoal creature has a mate.
She's delicate, she's tough: mauve, like a fleshy Caribbean flower.
They're family birds
and they're guarding a pure white egg.

How can you give up smoking
when a family of birds is nesting on your balcony?

The feathered creatures disturb her dreams.
A stranger's lips are touching her left ear.
He whispers – 'Do you know the meaning of your surname?
It means a net for capturing birds.'

She wakes with the dream still snagging,
caught up in the trammel of bedlinen.
She's feeling kissed, but was that kiss just a greeting?
She throws the net off, and exactly where
are her cigarettes?

Finally she can see them – they're under the empty balcony.
They're scattered, like the little sticks in the game of mahjong.
Did you know mahjong means sparrows?

Ancient candles at modern tables –
                         brand new couples, shy, un-
                                          stable.
Late enough to pray for luck.
                    Late enough to think it's love.

(Late enough for truth and trust. Late enough for truth and touch.)

Gentle light, eyes glimpsing eyes. Gentle light won't criticise.
Grave –
        as 'Here's to laughter, here's to dance.'
                            Here's to cheers and here's to chance.
Here's to phone light, being forgotten.
                    Here's to the moon – cream lace,
cream cotton.
Here's to home, to soften… gentler light, eyes meeting eyes.

Gentle light, bless this life.

It's just not safe to crave this glow. It's just not safe – I should know.
Yet intimate risks
               a whispered promise. Intimate is skin,
                            is honest.

(Late enough to praise close up. Late enough to think it's love.)

Late enough to let light leave.
                    Late enough to hear her breathe.
As if light was all the other senses, darkness lush with recompenses –
taste and touch and blush-warm scent.
                    As if this world were somehow meant.

    Late enough for truth and trust.
                Late enough to know it's love.

I woke and thought: *Her tattoo has shifted.* Last night, it covered the other shoulder.
I kissed your tattoo. *She is still here.* (I thought: *She is still here!*)

No, the tattoo had been on this shoulder. It was just a sensation (not a memory,
                                                                    a sensation).
I was intoxicated, but it wasn't alcohol – half the wine remained in the dim
                                                                    wine bottle.

The dim wine bottle sat on the bedside table, sulking. I kissed your tattoo.
I thought: I don't know the meaning of this inscription –
abstract? figurative? calligraphy?
I thought: I don't know the meaning of this… happiness. I am afraid. I am
afraid of you, of calling this 'happiness'.

It *is*, certainly, that word – but when you name it, well…
I tell you, do not name it.

Now I kissed you gently and you began to waken.
Then I thought — actually, I believe you were awake already,
or half-awake. Waiting to be kissed? to be wakened?
(I thought: I have been waiting to be wakened. I have waited to be kissed.
                                                                    I have hoped.)

I kissed you and you moved as if you were waking. I admit
I was hoping now to be kissed, that soft touch, that attentive touch,
and you turned and smiled and I smiled –
that look between us, the whole face open to the whole face –
and you kissed me,
we kissed.

(You have the most beautiful laugh, it's a full, joyous laugh,
but this was a time for just smiling.)

I remembered – last night – you'd been searching for my tattoos
(I have no tattoos). No, that was the dream.
I think I had only just been wakened from that dream.
Had you wakened me, then turned away?

(You were trying to locate my tattoos
(as in reality as in the dream: there could be no success in that quest,
but I was old-fashioned and believed I had the right to remain silent,
let the meticulous search begin).
You were kissing me gently, inhaling me,
you were looking at me – your look liked the look of me!

You were a new tracker of a creature – I knew that we both loved the creatures,
that we saw ourselves as creatures (some people don't love animals) –
and, that night, caressing was your way of hunting.

It's my way of hunting –
I had, just seconds earlier, in the dream, tracked down another tattoo
(in the dream your first one, green-blue, like reality's double,
was on your other shoulder – that must have been why, after I had woken,
I'd thought it had changed position).

Your second tattoo was a butterfly.
It was made to look like paper, origami but alive,
a delicate red butterfly (they say red is lucky in China), folded by skilled hands.
We were laughing because it always flitted away,
stopping here and there right across your fine skin, then up, off,
always a moment beyond.
I still put my lips to your skin, though I knew the butterfly had flitted on.

I thought: we are abstract, we are figurative, we are calligraphy.
But we are more than aesthetics.

I thought, the kiss is so powerful, you — are powerful.

We held each other closer –
I can't say if I held you closer first, or if you brought me tighter in, enclosed me.
We tenderly enclosed each other.
I looked down onto your shoulder and the tattoo had gone –
it had moved to the other side.

I think it is abstract.

You touched my shoulder and showed me your second tattoo, the paper butterfly.
It had finally settled – on me.
It was sore – tattoos have to involve pain – but beautiful.

They say 'beautiful' and 'butterfly' shouldn't really be used in poems, they're
not really poetry,
but they *are* a blurry anagram of each other –
I intend to bend the rules
(in this soft light 'beauty' misremembers 'butterfly' beautifully).

Well I couldn't kiss myself, so you put your lips to my tattoo, my new tattoo,
and the butterfly let you. Red, yes, a deep red, and red (they say) is very lucky
in China.)

In the cold light of day, I should regret last night.
In the cold light of day, I should deny delight.
In the cold light of day I should rationalise tenderness, exit, end all this,
I shouldn't try to delay
                in the cold light of day.

In the cold light of day, this is where it should end.
In the cold light of day, 'we'll still be friends'.
In the cold light of day, we shouldn't even speak. We should kiss – once (on
                                the cheek),
find
                no sweet nothings to say
                    in the cold light of day.

I don't believe
        in that freezing light.
I don't believe
        in wronging that right.
I can't leave
        when each photon is full on with praise.
You can't be seen
        any other way,
                even… in the cold light of day.

In the cold light of day, we're talk and touch and thinking.
In the cold light of day, you're wide awake – I'm still blinking.
Everything's funny and serious and warm.
    We're wise like the silent, we're babbling… like the new born!
Surely it will always
        be this way…
                in the cold light of day,
in the cold light of day,
in the new light of day.

Small

The pact, the plan – ink,
puncturing the skin. Haiku –
black. Small of the back.

Between the Shoulders

Zone I can't see: texts
only you can read. Speak! Read
my back back to me.

Elbow

Embrace's shepherd,
closing in, gathering bliss.
All hinges – on this.

Hemline

Edge of knowledge, edge of trust –
the last guessed unknown.

Blessed: flesh, ours alone.

Ankle Bracelet

-anklet-anklet-ank-let-anklet-anklet-anklet-anklet-anklet-catch-

She writes yes my voice, yes my eyes, yes, this all-of-me, speaking,
but she's only writing

He writes yes my voice, yes my eyes, yes, this all-of-me, speaking,
but he is only writing

They write
but they are only writing

(They write –
they are only writing)

She writes yes beneath the outer hem, your fingers 'smoothening'
but she is only writing

He writes yes my hair, ruffle-combing,
yes your fingers, nearly scratching,
(gentle – not actually scratching)
but he is only writing

She writes yes the little catch, your quick unfastening
but she is only writing

She writes my dress hitched up, right up – for a second a blinding –
but she is only writing

She writes yes lower, the lower hem, and yes your fingers, your kissing
but she is only writing

He writes
She writes

He writes yes the buckle, the zigger, the zigger unzagging
but he is only writing

All, she writes, all, she writes, equalling everything,
all she writes, meaning uncovering
but she is only writing

She writes
He writes

All, he writes, all, he writes, equalling everything,
all he writes, a rush of unclevering
but he is only writing

She writes yes my hands yes my lips yes my mouth opening, taking,
I'm taking you, she's thinking, ('Ah'm Claiming Yoo!'
as if pretend fighting!)
but she is only writing

He writes breathing, I, I am breathing
deeply, sharply,
I am gently
pushing, gently
pulling
I am brush-caressing, I am breathing
but he is only writing

She writes, it's a kind of singing,
I'm work-work-working
(you're work-work-working)
faster and faster –
I'm a diva in this dainty opera,

you're a diva in this dainty opera,
but she is only writing

and now let's just be slowing,
she writes, calm yourself,
we're slowing,
(she's teasing,
she's only writing)

He writes yes (yes is exactly what he is writing, though is that a sigh he's sighing?),
he is only writing

He writes and now I am crouching, my lips are low, my kisses are low, touching,
he adores that word 'low', but he is only writing

Yes she writes yes but will your tongue be dwelling
on the nub of my question?
Yes, she answers (she answers for him), your tongue will be dwelling
on the nub of my question!
I know this, you are thorough,
you'll be solicitous, you'll be gravely dwelling
on the nub of my question!
but she is only writing

I will dwell, he writes solemnly – laughing –
I will most certainly dwell
on the pulsing nub of your etcetera!
but he is only writing

She writes, my lips (*those* lips which are not true lips,
and that nub of my delicate etcetera) –
have been waiting, I have been waiting, waiting, waiting,

waiting,
waiting,
and she is only writing

I can sense 'there' here, she writes, continuing
I can sense 'there' here, she writes, doubly continuing
but she is only writing

There is a new word, is it an old word, 'juicening',
There is a new word, is it an old word, 'swollening'
I am delicious, she writes,
but she is only writing

You are delicious, he writes, flicker-licking, inhaling
And that mouth which is not a true mouth – now she is writing the writing –
      (please say nothing, please, no responding!)
that mouth is opening, opening, that mouth is certainly opening
but she is only writing

And my tongue (that tongue which is not a true tongue), (now he is fully
                                        responding),
is finding, pausing,
that tongue which is not a true tongue,
which is harder, which is larger,
that stupider tongue which is not a true tongue,
(but we have to be kind to the stupid)
that tongue which is not a true tongue
is –

he is only writing

They are writing
They are writing

They are writing
They are writing

She writes yes to your forthing-and-backing, to your froing-and-toing, your
                                                downing-and-upping,
(she is only writing)
He writes yes to your forthing-and-backing, to your froing-and-toing, your
                                                downing-and-upping,
(he is only writing)

They are writing
They are writing

He writes yes and I'm hearing –
it's a word
and it's not a word
but you are certainly not complaining
(he is only writing)

She writes yes and I'm hearing –
another word,
it's a different word, is it a word?
and I am sure you are not complaining,
but she is only writing

and they are shaking, they write, they write, they are shake-shivering-shaking,
they write that they are shaking, they are shake-shivering-shaking,
they write that they are finishing, finishing this writing,
they are writing and this is finishing
they are only writing

when will there be no writing?
when truly will there be no writing?

She is only writing
and now he is sleeping –
he is actually sleeping,
he falls so quickly

she is thinking
she is thinking she'd like to be sleeping
close,
close to him sleeping
(he is dreaming, he is dreaming happily and they are there already,
they are already together,
they have just been close, as close as a being can be
to another being)

and, no, now they are talking, gently talking, just before sleeping

They are finished with writing.

It's the day after the day after Christmas,
Do you mean the day after Boxing Day?

It's the day after the day after Christmas,
and I'm struggling

with this acoustic guitar. But it's so fresh –
like a pear that's been split in half,

and the house is all French polish
('wood medicine', my father calls it).

He's made me a book case (he's a little late),
and he tells me, he says:

Look, the bottom shelf,
you can use the bottom shelf for records,

but the rest of the *book* case –
well, that's for books.

And then he says to me,
well, he sings it really.

He says: *Are you sinister?*
Are you sinister?

Are you sinister?
Or are you… dextrous?

It's the day after the day after Christmas.
Do you mean the day after Boxing Day?

It's the day after the day after Christmas,
and I'm struggling

with this electric guitar, but it's so fresh –
like a, like a… spill… of electric-blue paint.

And I know it, but I can't feel it,
the sun – the sun is coming back again.

And I feel it, but I can't know it (I can't know it),
my old flame –

she, she's coming back again.
She's coming back.

You know, she used to sing to me?
(It was more talking really.)

She'd sing: *Are you sinister?*
Are you sinister?

Are you sinister?
Or are you… dextrous?

You don't know
             your own mind.
I don't know mine.
Scared is harsh tonight,
             harsh is too kind.

Privilege flies again,
millionaires carve.
Crows know their rights. Crows
won't starve.

Certain looks I remember,
riots, restlessness.
I sang close to tears —
nerves, I guess.

You don't know
             your own mind —
you used to read mine.
Scared is harsh tonight,
             harsh is too kind.

Tell me one last time
how you learned to sing.
I'm jealous of your past,
everything.

We have history,
a grown-up fairy tale,
that sign in the woods,
'Moon – For Sale'.

More images flicker,
a scar on your skin.
You're saying 'pleasure',
'lose', 'lose – to win'.

Tell me, one last time,
how you taught me to sing.
I can't remember the start,
anything.

I saw my double
twice this week.
He's afraid –
to speak.

Ghosts don't chat,
they just warn or chant.
'I'm a breath,' mine says,
or 'Can' or 'Can't.'

He sings your hardest things
(just to keep in touch) –
off by heart, you
mean that much.

I saw your double
twice this week.
You're twice alive,
twice unique.

Floods on the high road – the moon
   couldn't keep dry.
You couldn't trust a tree that night. The stars
   weren't safe in the sky.

Infants on the fire escapes – police
   hunt the rain down.
You couldn't chance the chill that night – soldiers,
   soldiers, hushing up the town.

We are not 'just friends'. We are not 'just friends'.
We are not friends. We are not 'just friends'.

'Escape to the north – a new country
   from a dying shell,'
You promised me peace that night,
   touched my cheek, wished me well.

You can be too polite – decorum
   affronts with a qualm:
hurricanes and holy war that night and still,
   still you stay calm.

We are not 'just friends'. We are not 'just friends'.
We are not friends. We are not 'just friends'.

You're a survivor, but there's damage in existence.
I couldn't risk a kiss that night. You wouldn't risk
resistance.

Floods on the high road – the moon
    can't keep dry.
You couldn't trust a tree that night. The stars
    weren't safe in the sky.

We are not 'just friends'. We are not 'just friends'.
We are not friends. We are not 'just friends'.

I'm not sure if this is a letter
or some disbelieving prayer.
When I sing I sing to you,
sheltering out there.
We're both solo – out of reach,
beyond repair.

We are not 'just friends'. We are not 'just friends'.
We are not friends. We are not 'just friends'.

The two girls were always singing

　　　　　　　singing,

　　　　　　　　　　　　(singing).

They'd play on the scrap of land we call the meadow.
There used to be sheep there, when it was safe.

The river's a smear now
but they'd still manage to ruin their shoes –

their father called them the Mud Twins, the Sisters Clay.

　　　　　　　　　　　'We are all the Family Clay.'

The girls would clatter into the house,
shoes like loaves of dirt

and they were still singing
singing! singing!

I used to ask them to stop. Forgive me, I used to

　　　　　　　shout at them: stop! Stop your NOISE!

(your nerves jangle, the whole place is just a scrap, you're hemmed, hemmed in)

(They were
　　　　　　singing.)
　　　　　　Stop! (I told them.)

                              Their father said, 'At least it keeps them
                              occupied.'

A background hum, but it isn't background – your nerves jangle, my nerves
                                                                      jangle

(it isn't background)

It used to be a meadow, the two girls
singing that beautiful,
singing,

singing that stupid that beautiful

                                        singing that stupid beautiful –

It wasn't background, it was a drone.

Everyone's an expert and it's not just fear.
The idea of young men and here's an intercept,
class system renewed –

in blood, boss.

Count the dead
by socio-economic caste. Work the silent and the silent work themselves.
You're thinking *Just look after your mates.*

I will be peaceful with you.

The idea of young women and an encased self for life,
controlled explosion. Man up,
girl. There are so many choices: put the kids' photos on the device /

point the device at the kids.

These are live experiments, unsold weapons on discount with a threat,
uranium's not a chemical, is it?
So a little respect for peacetime full force, that's solemn practice.

Where's your sad face for schools? Special stickers in the pack.

I am on the island today.
You can't come because we can't both afford it.
You can't come because you have to finish the Truewall contract.
You can't come because it's the century of buying wives on the supply island.
You can't come because it's the century of selling wives on the supply island.

You say I'm a 'shemale', that I, too, have my price; X is most certainly Y.
Complex equations are slippery on your tongue – you hiss them, you whisper
                                                  them, you kiss as if,
you kiss as if you don't want to know what you know. You overstand everything.

Your secrets are secret. You know I always
keep myself to myself, during a crossing.

                              *

I am on the island today.
You can't come because they don't allow wheelchairs
on any day with the word day in it.

English is the language of international law.

                              *

I am on the island today.
You can't come because that would be tourism.
You can't come because I'm missing you too much.
(They won't let me cash-in longing:
the machines just distribute sweetie wrappers,
birth certificates, IOUs –
all through gritted teeth.)

I am on the island today.
There is one bird here that is flightless.
It forages like a mouse, like an elderly man, like an elderly woman.
It forages like an elderly mouse, like a young man or a young woman,
all chewing chewing gum to concentrate.

It wears a heavy coat made of antique black feathers.
They're stitched but you can't see the thread.
We are ugly and we are perfect.

I am on the island today.
Come as fast, as fast,
as fast as –

I'd known her for years and the allergic reaction
    which reddened her face like an infection,
    raw, tender,
never alarmed me –
after all, I'd placed it there, with a movement of the hand.

With a deadpan look she'd leave a breast just exposed
and I'd say I enjoyed my visit, thanks for a lovely —.
I'd say I just popped in, but you're popping out,
        and fasten her robe, sing, 'All respectable again.'

Over the years, sorrowful affection, slapstick, repetition,
quite the picture.

I'd known her for years but not her children,
        (the boy has a bad eye)
                her affection for theatre.
There's a pattern to 'allergic reaction', a pattern to celebration.
It's all placed there,
    with a movement of the hand.
Women sometimes – in small groups – laugh together,
sorrowful affection, slapstick, repetition,
        (quite the picture).

At the beach a family – skin raw, tender –
    have known each other for years
    and then
        'all respectable again',
           thanks for a lovely —.
Remember old Alfred, that young dog panting,
and once,
    on the abstract white, there was diesel,
        like an infection?

I don't like 'white' and I don't like 'black':
white is mud, black's mud.
You touched and I
                    just looked.
You alarmed me – after all, who placed it there,
with a movement of the hand?
                              Who
                                    hunts us,
knows we're raw, beneath the last layer, hunting, tender?
Violent does the dirty work for Sentimental. You don't redeem an atrocity
with an atrocity.
We want to enjoy our visit.

Over the years, exposed, we are not children,
yet risk sharing affection
                          for a movement of the hand..
'Sleep with me,'
                  but you just dream of your father, raw, tender,
wake up with a deadpan look.
You're sipping your own 'gravy'. Is it alcohol or blood?
                                    quite the Battle of Hastings.
Remember old Harold, that young cat panting?
I'd come to know that creature for years and the allergic reaction
which reddened my face, an abstraction,
always alarmed me. You'd placed him there
                              with a movement of the hand.

You still say you're immune to the plague –
                        in the garden, touch and then just look.
Your radiance! and I remember
            an old Indian-style shirt,
                              buttonless and just loose.

Be open with me, expose me. After all, you've
known my memories for years,
              the family brambling, high jinks all over the disused line,
laughing together and now, alone.
You know how I bend.

There's a pattern to ceremony, but after all
just look at this single head,
                at this breast exposed,
                                at this breast exposed,
and as a matter of fact enjoy the visit, fancy a —?
Sorrowful affection, repetition, slapstick.
(Is the texture nationalism or self-determination? Is the colour
                                doors shutting or liberation?)
There's an exhaustion,
                women sometimes – in small groups.
They're asking, we're told, with a deadpan look, to be constrained.
Who hunts us?
Knows we're reddened beneath the last layer,
knows the movement, the aching repetition, this abjection to theatre.

Lucky you, a gated garden! – the politics of gravy, of alcohol, blood,
and their faces don't redden, it's a pattern, 'do it yourself' like a spill,
                                an awkward smudge,
but the invisible, in small groups, laugh at us together.
Repetition, slapstick, the affront of empathy, unbuttoning and just crude,
taxing every room essential for the new iron lung.

Look at this single head and dream of your father.
Men, sometimes, in small groups, laugh together, raw and tender,
                half confessions at the barbers,
and then 'all respectable again', asking, we're told, to be constrained – ties.

Remember the ceremonial party, kidstuff, pass the ice cream, musical jelly?
Over the years, we'd been… a pretend insurrection, revulsives,
	an affectation, an old-style umbrella,
		the louche loss of both glass slippers.
Is the rhythm pornography or is it erotica?
You make me sick! Flat duplication like reaction like infection like refraction,
flattening the glob, depassioned paste, puke even voidless.
Quite the picture.

(Snacking's my addiction, and opening my legs
		just wide enough on abstract white, in the animation.)

The boy has a bad eye,
	an accident with a music stand,
yet over the years a refined insect would know… how to enjoy herself,
		share see-through beneath petrochem's skyline.
You face it side-on, spread your apron
	like a bib, a mouthy pelican, and, sincere, gather to share.
Since we're small but hardly children
	the beach has been reddened in celebration.
It's the right place to allow exhaustion,
	it's the right place, deadpan, to lean on an adult, their idea.

No doubt, over the years, there will be
		sorrowful affection,
			masks and musicians, fruit and frets.
He's handling that industrial fish like a mandolin.
(Men, sometimes, in small groups, laugh together, grown-up children.)

She'd fastened her own robe, singing, 'All respectable now,'
					blue.
I don't wish I don't like naked, soft, to be open to touch.

I'd known her for years, but not her religion,
      narrow, but her songs! (her affection for theatre).
She danced with animation, frenzied footwork on the darkened crimson,
reddened and reddened.
'Girl' she called herself, in a triangular dress.
It was in the time of the rise of the cartoon in poetry, the politics of gravy.
Lacy top / black shawl / red smock –
              a religious mentor alarmed her, threatened to look after her,
raw and slapstick, quite the picture. She
did not enjoy the visit.
(The gated garden is open to all property owners in the exciting new development.)
Over the years she found the right place to enjoy celebration,
                      with masks and musicians, fruit and frets,
with a movement of the hand.
She'd fasten her own robe, singing, 'All respectable now,'
                                blue.

'Are you a man or a monkey-puzzle?'
(Chunks knocked out of him and new engineering for the body's casings.)
Men and women, sometimes, women and women, men and men,
                all welcome with the children in vast groups –
laughter and, over the years, *sorrowful affection, slapstick, abstraction.*
This is the time and place for a time and a place, a festival for practical dreams.

Over the years, radiance and see-through,
                  theatre in the raw, tender ties.
She'd fasten her own robe,
           blue.
Over the years, facing this facing,
             sorrowful affection, sorrow and affection,
sorrow and
      love, and all welcome,

all welcome, she'd
        fasten her own robe, thanks, blue. That blue robe!

(All welcome,
     sorrow and love,
          hands free,
              a movement of hands.)

Medicate to lessen what's intimate in sorrow,
or talk, talk it over –

    all this choice in reasons, in the render,
    and it's just between you and no-one in particular, a value one-to-one.

    Faith in a reflecting surface – I confess, no inner life to speak of
    and a thirst for outerness. From sip to gulp a zepto sec,
    so multiply. Still no quench.
    Sensation consumption, max and no check: where's that exteriority
                                 heading?

Para-diagnose and park it, self-drug.
In any case, less self, thanks, and a quest for structures of the collective.
I know, the good future's old-fashioned.
Belonging to sharing needs activation. It doesn't scratch a plan for let's get off
                                  this planet.
There's so much space, together.

A fine car pursuit, screech of post-production. Keep going. They're close, gaining.
They're close, shape-shifting,
like like to the function of like. They're

a liquid air acceptance, that kind of government.
The mobilised layers stuff mouths with all a bit harmless,
so much dust you don't see the pyroclastic flow –
viscose tides of it in the menace,
viscose tides of it in the confidence,
viscose, but they're saying just breathe this clothy slick in, it's
natural,

grab yourself a leg-up, grip justifies grasp, use your stealth, hot royalise.

Can this weight, this velocity, be used?
It doesn't start with choice, with the unit 'you', how anyone might feel.
Privilege polices the presets, trumpets its come-the-innocent equal opportunity
/ 'just join in'.

It's a way of lifestyle, a shield formation, the self-special,
aggrandised gangs hoarding elegance and 'give the hordes a kicking, example
serves'.

Etch a plan for let's get off this planet. There's so much inner space, out there,
together.

THE CLOUDS ARE SHIPS AND ISLANDS, THE MOUNTAINS ARE
ISLANDS AND SHIPS, ABOVE A CALM SOLID SEA

sky island   sky island sky island   sky island   sky island   sky island sky island

mountain islands   mountain islands   mountain islands
   m o u n t a i n i s l a n d s   m o u n t a i n i s l a n d s
   mountain islands   **mountain islands**
                              hilltop island   skyships
   skyships   **skyships**   skyships   **skyships**   skyships

skyships skyships skyships   **skyships   skyships   skyships**
                                      skyships skyships
f l a t   c a l m   t h e   w i d e   p l a i n
f l a t   c a l m   t h e   w i d e   p l a i n

viewpoint

Melancholy knows
        the interior of slow. Melancholy knows
                what it wants to know,
inertia yearning, waiting, longing,
            a quiet river's stepping stones,
a quiet river's undertow.

          Ribbons tacked to a shaking tree. Ribbons wracked,
                weather-bleached.
          Prayers and curses with their ink all run,
              'marriage, please,' 'save my son!'
          A quiet river flows right past, a quiet river
          to the last.

Thirst – at a rate of thou-shalt-nots.
Thirst – too late – for beauty spots.
Space,
       much more than all too much.
Space, too close,
            no speech, no touch.
A quiet river on the screen.
         A quiet river beyond belief.

Melancholy knows
        what it wants to know.
Melancholy knows
        the inside of slow,
            inertia yearning, waiting, longing,
a quiet river, a walk alone,
a quiet
     river's
        stepping
           stones.

In flight
      the weightless holdall
             of a jack-of-every-trade.

Opening, closing. Wrapped / Unwrapping. Sharp /
Frayed.

Black and white,
        not
            quite
            spilling the beak,
       (freak
           go-ahead scissors –
               red and double length, industrial strength).
                  Red legs
                    a drag,
                      long brittle tongs.

A bag – roughly stuffed –
           yet
              descends
                  with grace
(knows enough
        (technician's pride)),
               lands
precise.

MOONSHOT

gold visor and grey foil and silver foil

inverted bubbles the craters

hardened bubbles the huge all-face helmets
quarry dunes but no quarry

a blue baby

the first swirl of hair cloud white

grey / blue / grey / blue / grey / blue /

a blue old man a blue old woman

the last swirl of hair cloud white

the world brims
light
water

a tattoo
(like fronds)

fronds
(like a tattoo)

the world brims
the whole delta

childhood dams

light
water

lines the tide leaves
soft sand

lines linen leaves
soft skin

lines
leaves leave
(grass beneath one side of a face)

(you back then
me back then
sleeping)

'wake me' –
   a murmur, a dream –

'wake me' –
waking

laden light
weightless water

the world brims
(with the world)

THESE CHOICES ARE NOT CHOICES

Urgency, and these choices are not choices, are not urgent –
to cut your finger turning a page or to tire, squandering pumped light.
There is public private news and want want want – without fathomed angst.

The screen disowns its imperatives, I have been compulsed:
high frequency, low amplitude, a constant sub-pang for a friend and a dataset.
Or absence? Or absence? Absence or else?

This push not to be,
to be in your own absence. I

love our long hours enfolded: sending, receiving, sending, receiving.
No – 'thanks', 'praise', doesn't touch what touch is, each euphoric sense,
and I do say 'love' and I don't delete darkness.

We transmit a very short distance, and sometimes we read.

ACKNOWLEDGEMENTS

Some of these poems made earlier appearances in *Archipelago*, *The Arts of Peace*, *Codex* (Collective Investigations), *Ecstatic Peace News*, *Lighthouse*, *Magma*, *Nutshell*, *PN Review*, *P.O.W. Broadsheets*, *Rebus* (Rio de Janeiro), *Revista Luvina* (Guadalajara), and *The Times Literary Supplement*; as poems set to music in the albums *Just Good Friends* by Roberto Sainz de la Maza and *Age of Exploration* by Mirabeau; as poems for the Jaybird Productions performance *Beginning to See the Light*; and for the Poetry Library / Arts Council Collection project *Then One Day Something Happened*. Some were written when I was European Poet in Residence at the University of Coimbra and at the village of Monsanto, Portugal. My thanks to all those involved, and to those others who have encouraged me in the living and writing of this book, including Hannah Lowe, Donny O'Rourke, Peter McCarey, Anne Gutt, Iain Bamforth, and David Kinloch. Lastly, thank you so much Caroline Isgar for the specially made painting, this book's cover.